Elements of True Prayer

Elements of True Prayer

by
John MacArthur, Jr.

WORD OF GRACE COMMUNICATIONS
P.O. Box 4000
Panorama City, CA 91412

1988 by
JOHN F. MACARTHUR, JR.

Library of Congress Cataloging in Publication Data

MacArthur, John, 1939-
    Elements of true prayer / by John MacArthur, Jr.
      p.   cm. — (John MacArthur's Bible study)
    Includes indexes.
    ISBN 0-8024-5367-8
    1. Prayer—Biblical teaching. 2. Bible. O.T. Daniel IX, 1-19-
-Criticism, interpretation, etc. 3. Bible. N.T. Matthew VI, 9-10-
-Criticism, interpretation, etc. I. Title. II. Series: MacArthur,
John, 1939-   John MacArthur's Bible studies.
BS1199.P68M33   1988
248.3′2—dc19   88-12918
                                            CIP

1 2 3 4 5 6 Printing/LC/Year 92 91 90 89 88

Printed in the United States of America

Contents

These Bible studies are taken from messages delivered by Pastor-Teacher John MacArthur, Jr., at Grace Community Church in Panorama City, California. These messages have been combined into a 4-tape album entitled *Elements of True Prayer*. You may purchase this series either in an attractive vinyl cassette album or as individual cassettes. To purchase these tapes, request the album *Elements of True Prayer*, or ask for the tapes by their individual GC numbers. Please consult the current price list; then, send your order, making your check payable to:

WORD OF GRACE COMMUNICATIONS
P.O. Box 4000
Panorama City, CA 91412

Or call the following toll-free number:
1-800-55-GRACE

1
Elements of True Prayer—Part 1

Outline

Introduction
A. The Contribution of Daniel's Prayer
B. The Context of Daniel's Prayer
   1. Its biblical context
      a) The prayer's answer
      b) The prayer's antecedent
   2. Its historical context
      a) Concerning Darius (v. 1)
         (1) An indication of the date
         (2) The identity of Darius
            (*a*) The successor of Belshazzar
            (*b*) The son of Ahasuerus
            (*c*) A descendant of the Medes
            (*d*) The king of the Chaldeans
      b) Concerning Daniel (v. 2)
         (1) His age
         (2) His influence
         (3) His discovery
   3. Its spiritual context

Lesson
I. Prayer Is Generated by God's Word (vv. 2-3)
   A. The Principle Explained
      1. The sovereignty of God
      2. The responsibility of Daniel
   B. The Principle Illustrated
      1. Psalms 119
      2. Revelation 22
      3. Ezra 9

Introduction

The Holy Spirit governs the way God's Word reaches His people. People sometimes ask how I know what to teach. As I spend time in prayer, evaluate where the church is spiritually, and listen to the Spirit of God, it becomes clear what I should teach. The Lord opens my understanding and directs my choice.

Because God guides us in response to our prayers, we must not underestimate prayer's importance. Prayer is a frequent theme in Scripture, and I believe Daniel 9:1-19 is one of the greatest Old Testament passages on prayer.

A. The Contribution of Daniel's Prayer

Daniel 9 doesn't teach us how to pray. Instead, it is a model of majestic, inspiring prayer. It teaches about prayer through example.

Daniel set a standard of spiritual excellence in prayer, as well as in almost every other area of his life. He was a man with an unusual level of commitment. Daniel was uncompromising, bold, full of faith, unselfish, humble, completely resistant to the world around him, persistent in his commitment, holy and incorruptible, consistent, trustworthy, virtuous, obedient, and worshipful. In chapter 6 he demonstrated that he was a man of prayer—so much so that he kept his prayer times even though he knew that as a result he would be thrown into a den of lions. Even his prayer gives insight into his character. Daniel's deep sense of sinfulness was the outgrowth of his commitment to God. As we examine his prayer in chapter 9, we will see all the elements of true intercessory prayer.

B. The Context of Daniel's Prayer

1. Its biblical context

    a) The prayer's answer

    Daniel 9 records Daniel's prayer and God's answer. Although Daniel prayed for the restoration of the Jewish people to their land, God answered with the promise of the ultimate restoration of the Messiah. Although Daniel prayed at a particular time in his life, God answered with a statement that extended into the future. Perhaps God answered in such a magnanimous manner because of the virtue of the one who prayed.

    When people study Daniel 9, they usually emphasize God's answer—the seventy-weeks' prophecy, which details the arrival of the Messiah. But Daniel's prayer is the main thrust of the chapter, covering twice as many verses as God's answer. Prophecy is important, but it can never substitute for prayer. God never calls us to be so speculative and attached to the future that we lose sight of the present.

    b) The prayer's antecedent

    Daniel 9 doesn't follow chapter 8 in immediate chronological order. Daniel's organization is primarily thematic. Daniel's prayer in chapter 9 resulted from the fact that he "was sick . . . and . . . astonished at the vision" that he had seen in chapter 8. Having seen the terrible sweep of Gentile history with its oppression of Israel, Daniel became sick and faint. He was bearing such a heavy emotional and spiritual burden that he physically collapsed. Daniel's brokenness over what would happen to Israel is the logical connection to his prayer on behalf of his people. Perhaps that explains why the Holy Spirit put the content of chapter 9 after that of chapter 8.

2. Its historical context

   a) Concerning Darius (v. 1)

   "In the first year of Darius, the son of Ahasuerus, of the seed of the Medes, who was made king over the realm of the Chaldeans."

   (1) An indication of the date

   The events of chapter 9 occurred "in the first year of Darius," which was the same year as the events of chapter 6. Therefore this prayer may be similar to the ones Daniel prayed when he risked losing his life in the lion's den.

   (2) The identity of Darius

   (*a*) The successor of Belshazzar

   Darius is likely another name for Cyrus, the first great monarch of the Medo-Persian Empire. The Babylonian Empire ended in chapter 5 with the feast and drunken orgy of Belshazzar. The night of the feast the kingdom was taken from Belshazzar, fulfilling the prophetic handwriting on the wall (vv. 25-27). When the Medes and the Persians set up their kingdom (v. 28), the first Gentile power was replaced by the second, ruled by Cyrus. As a title, Darius can be translated "the holder of the scepter," referring to a king or sovereign.

   (*b*) The son of Ahasuerus

   Because Ahasuerus was a common name for kings at that time, we can't be sure of his identity.

(*c*) A descendant of the Medes

Although Cyrus was actually a Persian, as ruler of the Medo-Persian Empire he was considered to be a descendant of the Medes as well. He could apparently claim descent from both the Medes and the Persians, so he identified himself with both groups who had been amalgamated in the Empire.

(*d*) The king of the Chaldeans

The realm of the Chaldeans was the territory of ancient Babylon that was conquered by the Medo-Persians. And the first ruler of the Medo-Persians was Cyrus, evidently also called Darius.

b) Concerning Daniel (v. 2)

"In the first year of his reign I, Daniel, understood by [the] books the number of the years, concerning which the word of the Lord came to Jeremiah, the prophet, that He would accomplish seventy years in the desolations of Jerusalem."

(1) His age

Estimates of the date of this "first year" vary from 539 to 536 B.C. By that time Daniel would have been at least eighty years old. If he was taken to Babylon around fourteen years of age, by the first year of Darius he would have been in captivity approximately sixty-five years.

(2) His influence

Daniel was famous. Even though the Babylonian Empire had passed away, he maintained his position in the palace. When the Medes and the Persians heard about Daniel, a man who could interpret dreams and survive the lions' den, they were impressed. Daniel had acquired great wisdom through years of experience and exposure to

11

the law of God. Consequently he was God's special instrument.

(3) His discovery

Even though Daniel received divine revelation, he did not neglect his responsibility as a student of the Word of God. Through their years in exile at Babylon, the Jews apparently had acquired the scrolls of the Old Testament law, writings, and prophets. Perhaps they had been copied by scribes during the Exile and were available to Daniel. The set of books included the writings of Jeremiah, who had prophesied and recorded his prophecies prior to and immediately following the captivity of Judah. Daniel probably read from two passages in Jeremiah. Jeremiah 25:11-12 says, "This whole land [of Judah] shall be a desolation, and an horror; and these nations shall serve the king of Babylon seventy years. And it shall come to pass, when seventy years are accomplished, that I will punish the king of Babylon, and that nation, saith the Lord, for their iniquity, and the land of the Chaldeans, and will make it perpetual desolations." Jeremiah 29:10 says, "For thus saith the Lord, After seventy years are accomplished at Babylon, I will visit you, and perform my good word toward you, in causing you to return even unto this place."

As Daniel was reading, he read those remarkable prophecies in the Word of God and discovered that seventy years was determined for the captivity. Having longed for an end of Judah's captivity and their subsequent restoration to the land, he realized the captivity was nearly over. If the captivity began in 605 B.C. when Daniel was taken captive, it had lasted almost seventy years. Even if the dates for the second or third deportations were used, the end of the captivity was near. That marvelous discovery inspired Daniel's prayer. When he understood the Word of God, he began to pray.

3. Its spiritual context

Notice Daniel's attitude as he comes before God: "I set my face unto the Lord God, to seek by prayer and supplications, with fasting, and sackcloth, and ashes; and I prayed unto the Lord, my God, and made my confession, and said, O Lord, the great and awesome God" (Dan. 9:3-4). The spiritual context of Daniel's prayer is humility (v. 3), confession, and reverence (v. 4). Those three constitute the proper attitude of prayer—the kind of heart one is to have when he comes before God. The burden of Daniel's prayer was his own sinfulness and God's great and awesome majesty.

Let's examine the prayer itself, which shows us the nature of true intercessory prayer. There are eight important, timeless principles of prayer that should govern and guide our communion with God.

Lesson

I. PRAYER IS GENERATED BY THE WORD OF GOD (vv. 2-3)

"In the first year of his reign I, Daniel, understood by books the number of the years, concerning which the word of the Lord came to Jeremiah, the prophet, that He would accomplish seventy years in the desolations of Jerusalem. And I set my face unto the Lord God."

A. The Principle Explained

Daniel's prayer was born out of an understanding of the Word of God. That's why it's so important to study Scripture. If we don't understand God's Word, we can't understand His purposes and plans, which should govern and guide our prayers. When Daniel saw God's plan, he began to pray. In fact, I'm sure Daniel believed his prayer was part of the fulfillment of the Word of God itself.

1. The sovereignty of God

   Daniel recognized with certainty the divine purpose, fully believing in the sovereignty of God. Knowing the book of Jeremiah was the Word of God, Daniel was confident it would never be altered. Although he believed God would fulfill His Word, he still prayed.

   Human reason sometime questions the need to pray. After all, if God has decreed seventy years, why pray for deliverance sooner? Even though the relationship of prayer and sovereignty can't be fully comprehended, Daniel understood his responsibility to pray.

Do My Prayers Have Any Part in God's Sovereign Work?

We can never fully understand the relationship between God and man. I don't understand completely how God wrote the Bible using men as instruments, how God became a man and remained God at the same time, how I can be saved by my own choice and be chosen before the foundation of the world by God's sovereign will, or how God can sovereignly work while allowing my prayers to play a part. But it's neither necessary nor possible for us to understand those things.

2. The responsibility of Daniel

   When Daniel read the plan of God, he cried out in brokenness and penitence to God on behalf of his people rather than becoming fatalistic. His request, which he mentioned at the end of his prayer (v. 19), was simply, "Do; defer not." In other words, "Do what you've planned." God had already said what He was going to do. Daniel was simply pouring out his heart in recognition of God's will.

   We should pray when we discover God's purposes in His Word, not because God needs our prayers to perform His will, but because we need to line up with His causes. Prayer is for us. When we see our sinfulness and our need of His grace and power, we can submit ourselves to His plan.

B. The Principle Illustrated

1. Psalm 119

The psalmist said, "Thy testimonies also are my delight and my counselors" (v. 24). In other words, "When I read Your Word (testimonies), it becomes the counselor that instructs my mind." Such instruction is utterly necessary. Verses 99-100 say, "I have more understanding than all my teachers; for thy testimonies are my meditation. I understand more than the ancients, because I keep thy precepts." The psalmist was simply saying that if he wanted to know God's plans and understand His precepts, he would have to commit himself to God's Word. Prayer isn't asking God to change what He's going to do; it's identifying myself with His plans. Prayer and the Word are inseparably linked together, for I can't pray intelligently about His plans unless I understand what His Word says.

2. Revelation 22

Jesus said to the apostle John, "Surely, I come quickly" (v. 20). John responded, "Even so, come, Lord Jesus." John was identifying with the need for Christ to return.

3. Ezra 9

Ezra wrote, "Then were assembled unto me everyone who trembled at the words of the God of Israel, because of the transgression of those who have been carried away; and I sat appalled until the evening sacrifice" (v. 4). When the Israelites came back to the land under the leadership of Ezra and Nehemiah and heard why the Word of God said they were taken captive, they began to shake with conviction. Ezra himself said, "At the evening sacrifice, I rose up from my heaviness; and having torn my garment and my mantle, I fell upon my knees, and spread out my hands unto the Lord, my God, and said, O my God" (vv. 5-6). Ezra then launched into a prayer that grew out of his comprehension of the plans of God as revealed in His Word.

4. Nehemiah 8-9

"All the people gathered themselves together as one man into the street that was before the water gate; and they spoke unto Ezra, the scribe, to bring the book of the law of Moses. . . . And he read from it facing the street that was before the water gate from the morning until midday. . . . And Ezra, the scribe, stood upon a pulpit of wood, which they had made for the purpose. . . . And Ezra opened the book in the sight of all the people (for he was above all the people); and when he opened it, all the people stood up. . . . So they read in the book in the law of God distinctly, and gave the sense, and caused them to understand the reading" (Neh. 8:1, 3-5, 8). If you read further in Nehemiah, you will discover that in response they began to examine their own hearts, praising God and confessing before Him: "The children of Israel were assembled with fasting, and in sackcloth, and with earth upon them. And the seed of Israel separated themselves from all strangers, and stood and confessed their sins and the iniquities of their fathers" (9:1-2).

Again we see the same response: when the law of God was read, the people were driven to their knees. If you can read the Word of God and not be driven to prayer, you're not listening to what you're reading. Whatever we read should be cause for confession of sin, praise, or gratitude. Prayer and the Word are bound together. That's why the apostles committed themselves to both (Acts 6:4).

5. Ephesians 3

In Ephesians 3 Paul mentions his special ministry: "The dispensation of the grace of God which is given me toward you, how that by revelation He made known unto me the mystery . . . which in other ages was not made known unto the sons of men, as it is now revealed unto His holy apostles and prophets by the Spirit" (vv. 2-3, 5). After describing the mystery, he said, "For this cause I bow my knees unto the Father of our Lord Jesus Christ . . . that ye . . . may be able to comprehend . . . and to know the love of Christ" (vv. 14, 17-19). When Paul received the Word, it drove him to his knees.

The Word generates prayer because when it speaks of God, we long to commune with Him. When it speaks of blessing, we long to praise Him. When it speaks of a promise, we long to receive it. When it speaks of sin, it leads us to confess it. And when it speaks of hell, it leads us to pray for the lost. The Word of God causes prayer. Even though we know something is inevitable, we shouldn't fatalistically get up from our knees and walk away out of some kind of a sickly, theological indifference. Daniel's prayer, like all true prayer, began with an understanding of the Word of God.

II. PRAYER IS GROUNDED IN GOD'S WILL (v. 2b)

"The word of the Lord came to Jeremiah, the prophet, that He would accomplish seventy years in the desolations of Jerusalem."

A. Explained

Although God's will was clearly revealed, there was no sign of resignation on the part of Daniel. He believed prayer was part of its fulfillment. When God has a purpose, His people will identify with it. No Christian should ever pray as if he were changing the will of God. We pray to conform our hearts to His will, which is always to bless those who are obedient.

B. Illustrated

1. Revelation 6:10

The souls under the altar (possibly martyred saints from the Tribulation) are seen crying out, "How long, O Lord, holy and true, dost thou not judge and avenge our blood on them that dwell on the earth?" As I read that, I wondered why they didn't know how long. The Bible teaches that the Great Tribulation will last for three-and-a-half years. They could have read Daniel's prophecies, as well as the New Testament writings by that time, and known all of what God had planned for the seven years "of Jacob's trouble" (Jer. 30:7). So they may have known exactly how long, but they still longed for it to end. They were identifying with the injustice being done to God and hungered and thirsted for His will to be done.

2. 1 Samuel 12:19-25

"All the people said unto Samuel, Pray for thy servants unto the Lord thy God, that we die not; for we have added unto all our sins this evil, to ask for ourselves a king" (v. 19). Intent on having a king, the Israelites chose one for themselves. Realizing they had defied God, they begged Samuel to pray for them.

"Samuel said unto the people, Fear not: ye have done all this wickedness; yet turn not aside from following the Lord, but serve the Lord with all your heart. And turn ye not aside; for then should ye go after vain things, which cannot profit nor deliver; for they are in vain. For the Lord will not forsake His people for His great name's sake, because it hath pleased the Lord to make you His people" (vv. 20-22). "Moreover, as for me, God forbid that I should sin against the Lord in ceasing to pray for you" (v. 23). Samuel prayed because he was identifying with God's will for the people that they live within the blessing of the covenant.

"Only fear the Lord, and serve him in truth with all your heart; for consider how great things he hath done for you. But if ye shall still do wickedly, ye shall be consumed, both ye and your king" (vv. 24-25). The individuals who sinned would miss God's promises, but He would be faithful to the nation as a whole.

Even though Samuel knew the will of God was inevitable, he still recognized that failing to pray was sinful. A man of God prays in a way that is consistent with the will of God, not for God to change His will. I don't want what He doesn't want to give me. I want only His will to be done. That's not passive resignation; it's merely an honest statement of my desire. For example, even though I know Jesus will come at the hour determined by the Father, I find my heart praying, "Even so, come, Lord Jesus."

3. Matthew 26:39

Jesus was certainly not a fatalist. As He was nearing the cross, He asked in the garden, "O My Father, if it be possible, let this cup pass from me." He didn't want to have to endure God's wrath against sin and the consequence of fallen man if there were another way. Yet He said, "Nevertheless, not as I will, but as thou wilt." To pray for God's will is to pray that God will be honored, glorified, and exalted.

III. PRAYER IS CHARACTERIZED BY FERVENCY (vv. 3-4a)

A. Explained

Daniel portrays a magnificent picture of fervency in prayer. He didn't pray, "Lord, by the way, I have this thought I want to mention to You in passing." That's the way too many Christians pray. But Daniel said, "I set my face unto the Lord God" (v. 3a). He fixed his gaze on God. There was a passion, a persistence, and an intensity in his prayer. He said he sought the Lord "by prayer and supplications [extended petitioning], with fasting, and sackcloth, and ashes [the latter being cultural indicators of humility]; and [he] prayed unto the Lord, [his] God" (vv. 3b-4a). Although God had said the captivity would be seventy years, Daniel was fervent in his prayers.

B. Encouraged

1. 1 Thessalonians 5:17—Paul said, "Pray without ceasing." That's as fervent and persistent as you can be.

2. Luke 11:5-10—Jesus told a parable about a man who was persistently knocking on his friend's door to borrow some bread (vv. 5-7). The point of Jesus' story was that if a friend will meet your need because of your persistence (v. 8), how much more will God answer those who pray with great persistence (vv. 9-10, 13).

3. James 5:16—"The effectual, fervent prayer of a righteous man availeth much." That doesn't refer to our changing eternal plans. The changing occurs within us. The great value of prayer is how God uses it in us.

Daniel prayed with a resolute fervency unto the "Lord" (Heb., *adon*, "lord," "master"), signifying his submission to the sovereign authority of God. Yet, even with the knowledge that God is utterly sovereign, Daniel interceded for mercy.

The answer came in verses 20-21: "While I was speaking, and praying, and confessing my sin and the sin of my people, Israel, and presenting my supplication before the Lord, my God, for the holy mountain of my God; yea, while I was speaking in prayer, even the man, Gabriel, whom I had seen in the vision at the beginning, being caused to fly swiftly, touched me about the time of the evening oblation."

The constancy of Daniel's prayer is difficult for us to emulate. The thinking patterns of our society produce limited attention spans. For example, we watch half-hour television programs with thirty-second commercials. Such conditioning makes the art of meditation and persistence in prayer extremely difficult for us.

The Consequence of Seeking God

Daniel's prayer led him to fast and wear sackcloth and ashes. Why would a man with the character and integrity of Daniel be overwhelmed about his sin? Daniel knew God. A deep knowledge of God causes a deeper commitment and a greater sense of our sinfulness. Paul said he was the chief of sinners (1 Tim. 1:15). From our vantage point that seems like a ridiculous admission. But to Paul it was a reality because he saw his sin in all of its heinousness. So Daniel humbled himself as he came before God with his petitions.

Conclusion

The Lord is calling us to pray in these trying times. We tend to forget all the battles we're fighting today. Yet in the midst of the battles it's easy to sit in church and assume that no one needs our prayers. We may think that it's spiritual to say that when Jesus comes, everything will turn out right, but it's really fatalistic. We don't often pray with fervency and genuinely identify with the will and Word of God in the way Daniel did. Consequently, we miss intimate communion with God.

When you pray, it's not always necessary to come to God for an answer. Sometimes you can merely come with the weight of God's plan in your heart, seeking to be identified with His great and eternal purposes. If your theology hurts your prayer life, you have poor theology. But if you're studying the Word of God, the natural response is to commune with the God of the Word. It's impossible to be in the Word of God without being in communion with God. If your study of the Word doesn't produce communion, it's merely academic.

Prayer should be generated by the Word of God and grounded in the will of God. Rather than trying to force Him to do something, and demanding things from Him, God wants us to identify with His causes.

True prayer should also be characterized by fervency. Although I know that only a few will enter the narrow gate, and things in this world will continue to become worse, I still pray that God will be glorified and that souls will be saved. Daniel prayed that way even though he knew the prophecy.

Focusing on the Facts

1. What in Daniel 9 tends to attract people's attention away from Daniel's prayer? _____ is important, but it can never substitute for _____ (see p. 9).
2. What theme in chapter 8 motivated Daniel's prayer (see pp. 9-10)?
3. What major incident in Daniel's life probably occurred during the same year as his prayer in chapter 9 (see p. 10)?
4. Where did Daniel discover the prophecy? Explain the prophecy. Why would he be excited about it (see p. 12)?
5. What was the burden of Daniel's prayer (see p. 13)?
6. How does understanding God's Word affect our prayers (see p. 13)?
7. Why should we pray when we discover God's purposes in His Word (see p. 14)?
8. If we are not changing the will of God, why do we pray (see p. 17)?

9. Whose will did Jesus pray for in the Garden (Matt. 26:39; see p. 19)?
10. How did Daniel express his fervency in prayer (see p. 19)?
11. What principle does the story about a man wanting to borrow some bread teach (Luke 11:5-10, see p. 19)?
12. Why is the art of meditation and persistence in prayer so difficult for us (see p. 20)?
13. When we truly seek to know God, what will overwhelm us (see p. 20)?
14. When we fail to pray fervently, identifying with the will and the Word of God, what do we miss (see pp. 20-21)?

Pondering the Principles

1. Have you been guilty of fatalistic praying? Do you ever recall thinking, *What good is prayer going to do?* It's easy to let busyness crowd out personal communion with God, and when that happens, we lose the thrill of seeing God work in us. Instead, determine to be diligent in prayer. Have you prayed for your pastor, a missionary you know personally, a neighbor going through divorce, a friend whose father died, or the spiritual maturity of your husband, wife, or children? Try praying for requests on specific days. For example, on Mondays you could pray for your relatives and on Tuesdays for your pastor and church's ministries. The important thing is consistency. Make sure you follow up on those you are praying for. Nothing is more encouraging than seeing God work in a person for whom you have been praying.

2. If you can read the Word of God and not be driven to prayer, you're probably not listening to what you're reading. Have you ever been on a Bible-reading schedule and found yourself rushing through your daily assignments just to keep up? Approach the Bible more meditatively. Pause and consider what you have read. Take time to thank God for His truth, confess sin, or ask Him to enable you to apply what you've read. Remember that prayer and the Word are bound together. Avoid approaching the Bible merely from an academic standpoint, which prevents its impact in your life.

3. Read again 1 Samuel 12:24-25. Why should we "fear the Lord, and serve him" (see p. 18)? Meditate on what God has done in your life. Also read Psalm 103:1-2 and 1 John 4:9-10. Memorize one of those passages and thank God for "all his benefits" to you.

2
Elements of True Prayer—Part 2

Outline

Introduction

Review
I. Prayer Is Generated by the Word of God (vv. 2-3*a*)
   A. The Principle Explained
      1. The sovereignty of God
      2. The responsibility of Daniel
   B. The Principle Illustrated
II. Prayer Is Grounded in the Will of God (v. 2*b*)
   A. Explained
   B. Illustrated
III. Prayer Is Characterized by Fervency (vv. 3-4*a*)
   A. Explained
   B. Encouraged

Lesson
IV. Prayer Is Realized in Self-Denial (v. 4*a*)
   A. Exemplified
      1. In Daniel
      2. In the publican
      3. In Abraham
      4. In Isaiah
      5. In Paul
      6. In John
   B. Applied
V. Prayer Is Identified with God's People (vv. 5-16)
   A. The Principle Established
      1. By Paul
      2. By Samuel

Introduction

Daniel 6:10-11 clearly reveals what caused Daniel to be cast into the lion's den: "When Daniel knew that the writing was signed, he went into his house; and his windows being open in his chamber toward Jerusalem, he kneeled upon his knees three times a day, and prayed, and gave thanks before His God, as he did previously. Then these men assembled, and found Daniel praying and making supplication before his God." One of the elements of Daniel's great spiritual strength was his commitment to prayer.

In the book of Daniel the marvelous traits of Daniel's character unfold in an unassuming way. One such trait was his commitment to prayer. Daniel understood that prayer was living in the presence of God, and neither threats of death nor the loss of reputation or position could change his commitment. Prayer was his vital link with God. His persistence was similar to that of Jacob, who, when wrestling with the angel of the Lord, would not let him go until God had blessed him (Gen. 32:25-28; cf. Hos. 12:4). Daniel prevailed in prayer against the edict of the king in chapter 6, and in chapter 9 he prevailed in prayer in the midst of a crisis situation in the life of his nation.

The intercessory prayer of Daniel is a model for our praying. Such influence is fitting because Daniel's life constantly flowed in the vein of prayer. The influence of prayer has been noted by other great men of God. Nineteenth-century American evangelist D. L. Moody said, "Those who have left the deepest impression on this sin-cursed earth have been men and women of prayer" (*Prevailing Prayer* [New York: Revell, 1885], p. 7). It was said of Robert Murray McCheyne, a Scottish minister of the last century, that while he "did set apart special seasons for prayer and fasting, the real secret of his soul's prosperity lay in the daily enlargement of his own heart in fellowship with God" (*Memoirs of McCheyne*, Andrew A. Bonar, ed. [Chicago: Moody, 1948], p. xx). If it is true that those who have made the greatest impact on the earth have been people of prayer, we would expect Daniel to be a man whose life breathes and flows in prayer. That is precisely what we find in Daniel 9.

There are two basic problems with our praying: we often don't pray enough (cf. 1 Thess. 5:19) and we often don't know what to pray for (cf. Rom. 8:26). Studying Daniel's prayer will show us Daniel's fervency and the devout character of his intercession.

Review

In the first year of the Medo-Persian Empire, Daniel read the prophecy of Jeremiah that the captivity of the Jews would end after seventy years. Realizing that he had been in captivity for nearly seventy years, Daniel knew the prophecy's fulfillment was imminent. His discovery was immediately followed by his prayer, which illustrates the elements of true prayer.

I. PRAYER IS GENERATED BY THE WORD OF GOD (vv. 2-3*a*; see pp. 13-17)

A. The Principle Explained

1. The sovereignty of God

Daniel didn't indifferently resign himself to the sovereignty of God. He was convinced that God's sovereignty would bring to pass what God had preordained—but not without human choice.

What Do We Mean When We Say "Amen"?

Our prayers should agree with what we know God will do. That's the purpose of "amen" in the Bible. It means "so let it be." When we say to God, "Bring it to pass," or, "Let it be," we are asking that God's will be done.

God's Sovereignty—The Long and the Short of It

There have been times when God has extended situations and other times when He has shortened them. He lengthened the time of His patience with Israel, for the first time Christ came He was rejected. Although His earthly kingdom was postponed, God will yet restore and redeem His people Israel (Rom. 11:26). Because God is sovereign, we cannot restrict His will.

2. The responsibility of Daniel

Daniel began to pray, asking God to end the chastening. His praying grew out of an understanding of the Word of God. We also have the responsibility to pray. Jesus told His disciples to "watch and pray" (Matt. 26:41), and Peter exhorted his readers to "watch unto prayer" (1 Pet. 4:7). Those commands mean we must keep our eyes open to perceive what's happening so that we can pray specifically for needs. When you observe the world, the church, Israel, and the events that relate to each of them, you must be able to analyze what you see in the light of the Word of God, or you won't understand God's purposes in history or be able to pray intelligently.

B. The Principle Illustrated

Nehemiah prays in Nehemiah 1:11, "O Lord, I beseech thee, let now thine ear be attentive to the prayer of thy servant, and to the prayer of thy servants, who delight to fear thy name; and prosper, I pray thee, thy servant this day, and grant him mercy in the sight of this man. For I was the king's cupbearer." Having heard that the city of Jerusalem was in ruins, Nehemiah prayed knowing that Jerusalem was God's beloved city. What he saw was filtered through his knowledge of God's Word.

Likewise, we can never understand what is happening apart from the context of the Word of God. Daniel analyzed God's chastening of Judah by pagan nations when the Word of God was opened to him, and that analysis drove him to prayer. The better we understand God's Word, the better we can correctly analyze our circumstances and conform our prayers to what God has decided. People who know the Bible are people of profound prayer. Apart from the Word of God, our prayers are only shallow and meaningless words.

II. PRAYER IS GROUNDED IN THE WILL OF GOD (v. 2b; see pp. 17-19)

A. Explained

Daniel wanted God to bring His will to pass (cf. v. 19). Such praying is according to the will of God. John said that "if we ask anything according to his will, he heareth us; and . . . we know that we have the petitions that we desired of him" (1 John 5:14-15). This is how Jesus taught His disciples to pray: "Our Father, who art in heaven, hallowed be thy name. Thy kingdom come. Thy will be done" (Matt. 6:9-10). Prayer's function isn't to change the mind of God. God already desires the very best for us. Prayer brings us into agreement with His will, which is already the best.

B. Illustrated

Sometimes we don't know God's will. That's why Romans 8:26 says, "Likewise, the Spirit also helpeth our infirmity; for we know not what we should pray for as we ought."

The Will of God Identified

Although we can't know what God's will is in every situation, when we study the Word of God, we can learn what it is in some cases. The Bible tells us God's will for every believer.

- To be saved (1 Tim. 2:4)
- To be Spirit-filled (Eph. 5:18)
- To be sanctified, abstaining from sexual immorality (1 Thess. 4:3)
- To be submissive to the powers ordained by God (1 Pet. 2:13)
- To be thankful (1 Thess. 5:18)
- To be willing to suffer (for well-doing rather than evil-doing, 1 Pet. 2:15)

But when the subject of my prayer doesn't fall into one of the previous categories, and I don't know how to pray according to God's will, "the Spirit himself maketh intercession for us with groanings which cannot be uttered [divine communion between the Spirit and the Father]. And he [the Father] that searcheth the hearts knoweth what is the mind of the Spirit, because he maketh intercession for the saints according to the will of God" (vv. 26-27). When I don't know God's will, the Holy Spirit prays on my behalf. That's why "we know that all things work together for good" (v. 28). My primary prayer is that God do His will.

III. PRAYER IS CHARACTERIZED BY FERVENCY (vv. 3-4*a*; see pp. 19-20)

A. Explained

B. Encouraged

Expressions of Fervency in Prayer

- Wearing sackcloth (Neh. 9:1)
- Sitting in ashes (Job 2:8)
- Shaving the head (Job 1:20-21)
- Smiting the breast (Luke 18:13)
- Crying (1 Sam. 1:9-10)
- Throwing dust on the head (Josh. 7:6)
- Tearing garments (2 Kings 19:1)
- Fasting (Deut. 9:18)
- Sighing (Ps. 12:5)
- Groaning (Ps. 6:4-6)
- Loud crying (Heb. 5:7)
- Sweating blood (Luke 22:44)
- Agony (Luke 22:44)
- A broken heart (Ps. 34:18)
- A pouring out of one's heart (Lam. 2:19)
- Rending the heart (Joel 2:12-13)
- Making an oath (2 Chron. 15:12-15)
- Making sacrifices (Judg. 20:26)

These expressions of fervency were not limited to men. Hannah poured out her heart and would not eat because of the grief about her barrenness (1 Sam. 1:8). Having to risk her life, Esther said, "Go, gather together all the Jews who are present in Shushan, and fast ye for me, and neither eat nor drink three days, night or day; I also, and my maidens, will fast likewise, and so will I go in unto the king, which is not according to the law. And if I perish, I perish" (Esther 4:16).

Lesson

IV. PRAYER IS REALIZED IN SELF-DENIAL (v. 4a)

"I prayed unto the Lord, my God, and made my confession."

A. Exemplified

1. In Daniel

The heart of all true prayer is an awareness that we don't deserve to be in the presence of God. We have

31

nothing to commend ourselves to Him. Daniel began with the recognition of this reality as his confession shows. He knew that because of his sin nature, he didn't belong in God's presence. Daniel probably confessed many things in his heart, having searched his life and found everything that stood between himself and God (e.g., deafness to God's voice, disobedience to His commands, contempt of the sovereign lordship of God). Awareness of his sin brought Daniel to humility.

2. In the publican

The prayer of the publican in Luke 18:13 reflects the attitude of humility. But contrast it with the prayer of the Pharisee, who said, "God, I thank thee that I am not as other men are. . . . I fast twice in the week; I give tithes of all that I possess" (vv. 11-12). God didn't listen to that prayer because it was self-righteous and self-seeking.

3. In Abraham

When Abraham tarried before God in Genesis 18:27, he said, "Behold now, I have taken upon me to speak unto the Lord, who am but dust and ashes."

4. In Isaiah

Isaiah envisioned God "high and lifted up" (Isa. 6:1) and exclaimed, "Woe is me! For I am undone" (v. 5).

5. In Paul

The apostle Paul recognized that he had no right to be in God's presence. He even identified himself as the chief of sinners (1 Tim. 1:15).

6. In John

When John saw the majestic beauty of the ascended Christ, he fell before Him in humility (Rev. 1:17).

B. Applied

A lack of self-denial will produce impotence in your prayer life. Self-denial is setting your will aside for God's. If you're trying to badger God to do what you want you're not practicing self-denial. It's practically impossible to minister to anyone else through prayer, preaching, or other means until we take the path of self-denial. Knowing the importance of self-denial, Daniel dealt with the issue of pride and humility early in his life.

V. PRAYER IS IDENTIFIED WITH GOD'S PEOPLE (vv. 5-16)

Daniel started with himself ("I . . . made my confession"), but he didn't stop there. Notice that he uses plural pronouns, showing that he identified himself with God's people: "We have sinned" (v. 5), "neither have we hearkened" (v. 6), "O Lord, righteousness belongeth unto thee, but unto us confusion of face" (v. 7), "we have sinned" (v. 8), "neither have we obeyed" (v. 10), "yea, all Israel has transgressed thy law . . . therefore, the curse is poured upon us . . . we have sinned against him" (v. 11), "he spoke against us . . . our judges that judged us" (v. 12), "we have sinned, we have done wickedly" (v. 15), "our sins . . . our fathers . . . a reproach to all that are about us" (v. 16).

A. The Principle Established

1. By Paul

The Ephesians were to be "praying always . . . for all saints; and for [Paul]" (Eph. 6:18-19). The focus of our prayers is to be others. When we pray, we must realize that we don't deserve to be there. Then, as we seek the will of God, setting our own aside, we begin to pour out our hearts on behalf of others.

Daniel saw himself bound up in the lives of others. It was important for each Israelite to see himself as part of the nation. That is also necessary in the Body of Christ. First Corinthians 12:12 says that "the body is one." Verse 26 adds, "Whether one member suffer, all the members suffer with it; or one member be honored, all the members rejoice with it."

2. By Samuel

First Samuel 12:23 says, "God forbid that I should sin against the Lord in ceasing to pray for you." I learned long ago that I should not be the focal point of my prayers. When I recognize God's will, I forget myself and pray for others. Christians miss the purpose of prayer when their prayers dwell on "I, me, and mine." They're not embracing the needs of God's people.

B. The Perspective Explained

Paul always prayed for others. He never made a habit of praying for himself. When he did want prayer for himself, he asked someone else to do it (Eph. 6:19; 2 Thess. 3:1). I believe that is biblical. I don't need to be busy praying for myself. The Lord's model for prayer says, "Give *us* this day *our* daily bread. And forgive *us* *our* debts. . . . And lead *us* not into temptation" (Matt. 6:11-13, emphasis added). That shows us our prayers are to encompass the needs of one another. The Lord's Prayer is not a private, personal way for us to receive God's gifts.

1. We should intercede for others

   a) Galatians 6:2—Paul said, "Bear ye one another's burdens, and so fulfill the law of Christ." Jesus presented that law to His disciples in John 13: "A new commandment I give unto you, that ye love one another" (v. 34).

   b) Philippians 1:4—"Always in every prayer of mine for you all making request with joy."

   c) Colossians 1:3—"Praying always for you."

   d) Philemon 4—"Making mention of thee always in my prayers."

   e) 2 Corinthians 1:11—"Ye also helping together by prayer for us." Prayer is a mutual ministry of sharing.

f) 1 Timothy 2:1-2—We are to pray "for all that are in authority" over us.

g) James 5:14-16—We are to pray for those in need.

2. We should identify with others

As Daniel prayed for his people, he included himself in their sins and failures. He didn't stand apart as though he were righteous. A self-righteous man would have refused to identify with chastened sinners (Mark 2:16-17). Daniel could have said he was not a part of sinful Israel. After all, he had remained true to God for nearly eighty years. But Daniel embraced them because they were his people, and he knew he had sinned. Therefore, he wasn't ashamed to identify himself with their needs. Daniel understood the unity of Israel; we must understand that about the church as well.

Daniel passionately interceded for his people. His New Testament counterpart, Paul, prayed so intensely for the salvation of Israel that he wished himself "accursed from Christ" (Rom. 9:3) if that were necessary for them to be saved. What a marvelous example of concern for others! The key to intercession is identification, a spirit that says "we" rather than "I." Our prayers should never be directed toward ourselves without regard for how others will be affected. We should pray for what is best for the whole Body of Christ.

VI. PRAYER IS STRENGTHENED IN CONFESSION (vv. 5-15*a*)

A. The Need of Confession

Daniel didn't accuse his people of sin and claim that he himself was righteous. He knew he was a sinner. In verse 20 he says, "I was speaking, and praying, and confessing my sin and the sin of my people, Israel." His whole prayer is confession. When God is working in a life, repentance and confession will result. In fact, the truer your commitment to Christ and the deeper your love for God, the greater will be your sense of sinfulness. The closer we become to God, the more heinous our sins become.

B. Some Examples of Confession

1. David

   After David committed his terrible sins, he was nearly crushed with guilt because in the past he had walked with God as a man after God's own heart. His adultery with Bathsheba and murder of Uriah drove him to the marvelous confession of Psalm 51, where he said, "Wash me thoroughly from mine iniquity, and cleanse me from my sin" (v. 2).

2. The Jews

   a) Under Ezra

   In Ezra, the people became aware of their sins after committing themselves to God. As a result they were overwhelmed with their guilt and poured out their confession (chaps. 9-10).

   b) Under Nehemiah

   Nehemiah records an account of conviction by the Word of God in chapter 8, which produced the confession of their sinfulness in chapter 9.

3. Paul

   When Paul really understood the law of God and its unattainable standards, he said, "The commandment came, sin revived, and I died" (Rom. 7:9). Although confession should be a daily part of the life of a godly man or woman, an unprecedented realization of one's guilt before God will prompt it.

4. Jeremiah

   In Jeremiah 3, 8, 14, and Lamentations 1, Jeremiah cries out in confession to God, sensing the imminence of coming judgment by the presence of God.

5. Isaiah

When Isaiah saw the Lord "high and lifted up" (Isa. 6:18), surrounded by seraphim (v. 2) who cried "Holy, holy, holy" (v. 3), he began his confession by saying, "Woe is me!" (v. 5).

C. An Examination of Confession

1. Daniel's confession

   a) Acknowledging sin (vv. 5-8, 10)

   (1) Disobeying God's Word (v. 5)

   "We have sinned, and have committed iniquity, and have done wickedly, and have rebelled, even by departing from thy precepts and from thine ordinances."

   Those four phrases mean respectively that the Jews were guilty because they had missed the mark or wandered from the path, acted perversely, carried out premeditated evil, and defied authority. Those four different aspects of sin indicted the Jews from every possible angle.

   (2) Ignoring God's prophets (v. 6)

   "Neither have we hearkened unto thy servants, the prophets, who spoke in thy name to our kings, our princes, and our fathers, and to all the people of the land."

   In other words, "We didn't listen to Your spokesmen. We went our own way, not heeding the call."

   (3) Sensing their shame (v. 7; cf. v. 8)

   "O Lord, righteousness belongeth unto thee, but unto us confusion of face."

"Confusion of face" refers to their being shame-faced. Their hearts were so filled with shame that it showed on their faces. They were ashamed because they had once been a great people but had been reduced to outcasts and refugees. The Northern Kingdom had gone into captivity under Assyria, never to return. The Southern Kingdom had more recently been carried away to Babylon. Others had fled to Egypt when Gedaliah was assassinated (Jer. 41:2; 43:4, 7). God scattered Judah because of her treacherous sins. Consequently, the kings, princes, and fathers were all ashamed.

(4) Making no response (v. 10)

"Neither have we obeyed the voice of the Lord, our God, to walk in his laws, which he set before us by his servants, the prophets."

b) Accepting responsibility (v. 11)

"Yea, all Israel has transgressed thy law, even by departing, that they might not obey thy voice; therefore, the curse is poured upon us, and the oath that is written in the law of Moses, the servant of God, because we have sinned against him."

In Deuteronomy 28:15 God promises Israel that curses would be the consequence of disobedience. God faithfully kept His Word, whether blessing or punishment. Shame and judgment came because God said it would if the Israelites didn't obey. God's guarantee to punish disobedience points out one of the most important elements of confession: When God chastens you for sin, accept responsibility for that chastening and never blame God. There are always people who have blamed God. When confronted with his disobedience, Adam said, "The woman whom thou gavest to be with me, she gave me of the tree, and I did eat" (Gen. 3:12b). Adam in effect said, "I didn't ask to be married. You gave me this woman. I didn't even know what a woman was. Now you're holding me accountable for this sin?" Adam tried to shift responsibility for his sin to God.

As the judgment of the Tribulation begins, unbelievers upon the earth will blaspheme God (Rev. 16:21; cf. 6:16), denying any responsibility. People often ask how there can be a God when there is so much disaster in the world. They conclude that if there is a God, He must be cruel. Such people refuse to accept the fact that there are evil consequences in the world because the world is filled with evil men, who bring those consequences upon themselves.

c) Analyzing the consequences (vv. 12-15)

(1) Captivity (v. 12)

"He hath confirmed his words, which he spoke against us, and against our judges that judged us, by bringing upon us a great evil; for under the whole heaven hath not been done as hath been done upon Jerusalem."

From Daniel's perspective nothing had ever happened that was as disastrous as the captivities of Judah and Israel. But it happened just as God had said it would if His people didn't obey. They had been warned, so they couldn't blame God.

(2) Stubbornness (v. 13)

"As it is written in the law of Moses, all this evil is come upon us; yet made we not our prayer before the Lord, our God, that we might turn from our iniquities, and understand thy truth."

Daniel kept referring to what God had told Israel in the law of Moses—they had fair warning. When we sin and then receive the consequences we shouldn't blame God. He doesn't accept that responsibility. Sin has consequences. Daniel added that even when the pain came, they still didn't repent of their sins, confessing them and seeking God's forgiveness.

(3) Chastening (v. 14)

"Therefore hath the Lord watched upon the evil, and brought it upon us; for the Lord, our God, is righteous in all his works which he doeth; for we obeyed not his voice."

All negative circumstances and chastenings that result from sin are deserved because of our sinfulness. That is a mature perspective.

(4) Guilt (v. 15)

"Now, O Lord, our God, who hast brought thy people forth out of the land of Egypt with a mighty hand, and hast gotten thee renown, as at this day; we have sinned, we have done wickedly."

True intercessory prayer, then, is generated by God's Word, grounded in God's will, characterized by fervency, realized in self-denial, identified with God's people, and strengthened in confession.

Focusing on the Facts

1. What was one of the elements of Daniel's great spiritual strength (see p. 26)?
2. What does it mean to "watch unto prayer" (1 Pet. 4:7)? What is the only way we can pray intelligently (see p. 28)?
3. What does it mean to pray according to the will of God (see p. 29)?
4. What assistance do we have when we don't know "what we should pray for as we ought" (Rom. 8:26; see p. 30)?
5. What is the awareness we must have before we pray (see p. 31)?
6. What, in the text of Daniel's prayer, shows how he identified himself with his people (see p. 33)?
7. Apart from God, who should be in the focal point of our prayers (see p. 33)?
8. Why was Daniel quick to include himself in his prayer (see p. 35)?

9. What theme is emphasized throughout most of Daniel's prayer (see p. 35)?
10. The truer your commitment to Christ and the deeper your love for God, the greater will be your sense of _____ (see p. 35).
11. Why were the Jews terribly ashamed (see p. 38)?
12. Why are there evil consequences in the world (see p. 39)?
13. What in verse 13 shows that the Jews had been given fair warning (see p. 39)?
14. God's retribution demonstrates which of God's attributes (Dan. 9:14; see pp. 39-40)?

Pondering the Principles

1. Have you been searching for God's will for your life? On page 30 there are several aspects of God's clearly revealed will. Look up each of the references to make sure you understand it. Are you following His will that has already been revealed? If so, regardless of your location or circumstances, you are in God's will.

2. What caused the biblical characters listed on pages 36-37 to confess their sinfulness? When you realize something you're doing is wrong, what are your reactions? Do you sense before that it doesn't seem to fit into God's will? Are you hesitant to find out what the Bible says, fearing that you might be pursuing a wrong course of action? Do you believe David would have confessed by himself had he not been confronted by the Word of God through Nathan the prophet (see 2 Sam. 12:1-12)? Since the heart is so "deceitful above all things, and desperately wicked" (Jer. 17:9) that no one can know it—including ourselves—isn't it possible for us to sin and rationalize its heinousness? What does Hebrews 4:12 say is an effective tool for revealing our sin? Allow God to examine your life through His Word.

3
Elements of True Prayer—Part 3

Outline

Introduction

Review

I. Prayer Is Generated by the Word of God (vv. 2-3*a*)
II. Prayer Is Grounded in the Will of God (v. 2*b*)
III. Prayer Is Characterized by Fervency (vv. 3-4*a*)
IV. Prayer Is Realized in Self-Denial (v. 4*a*)
V. Prayer Is Identified with God's People (vv. 5-16)
VI. Prayer Is Strengthened in Confession (vv. 5-15)
   A. The Need of Confession
   B. Some Examples of Confession
   C. An Examination of Confession
      1. Daniel's confession (9:5-15)

Lesson
      2. Other confessions
         a) Joshua 7:19-26
         b) 1 Samuel 4-6
            (1) The context
            (2) The capture
            (3) The consequences
               (*a*) The destruction of Dagon
               (*b*) The punishment of the Philistines
            (4) The confession
VII. Prayer Is Dependent on God's Character (vv. 4, 7, 9, 15)
   A. God's Character Displayed in Daniel's Prayer
      1. Power (v. 4*a-b*)
      2. Majesty (v. 4*b*)

Introduction

Daniel 9 shows us that prayer is primarily communion with God. It's not so much designed for us to receive what we ask for as it is to identify ourselves with the Lord and His purposes.

Review

Having discovered God's plan for Israel while reading the book of Jeremiah, Daniel prayed, desiring to identify with God and what He promised to do. In his wonderful prayer, eighteen verses of preparation precede his petition. Implied in those verses are eight elements that mark genuine intercessory prayer.

I. PRAYER IS GENERATED BY THE WORD OF GOD (vv. 2-3*a*; see pp. 13-17)

Our prayer lives are the product of our study of God's Word. We go to the Word to find out what God is doing so we can pray intelligently.

II. PRAYER IS GROUNDED IN THE WILL OF GOD (v. 2*b*; see pp. 17-19)

Prayer is not trying to change God's mind but identifying with what He is already planning to do.

III. PRAYER IS CHARACTERIZED BY FERVENCY (vv. 3-4*a*; see pp. 19-20)

Prayer is passionate involvement in what concerns the heart of God.

IV. PRAYER IS REALIZED IN SELF-DENIAL (v. 4*a*; see pp. 31-33)

True prayer begins with a recognition of our unworthiness to come before God.

V. PRAYER IS IDENTIFIED WITH GOD'S PEOPLE (vv. 5-16; see pp. 33-35)

In true intercessory prayer we set self aside and become lost in the needs of others.

VI. PRAYER IS STRENGTHENED IN CONFESSION (vv. 5-15)

A. The Need of Confession (see p. 35)

Daniel's prayer was essentially a confession (cf. 4*a*). Confession merely means to say the same thing that God is saying about your sin, agreeing with Him that your sin is indeed your sin. True prayer enters the presence of God with a sense of God's absolute holiness and therefore is willing to acknowledge its own sin. Confession acknowledges we don't deserve to be in God's presence except by the righteousness of Christ, which covers us (2 Cor. 5:21; cf. Heb. 10:19-20).

Confession: The Preparation for Intercession

One writer said that before he began to pray for anything he would pray, "Give me a horror of sin, a dread of its approach, a deeper repentance; help me to chastely flee it and jealously to resolve that my heart shall be Thine alone. . . . Plow deep in me, great Lord, heavenly husbandman, that my being may be a tilled field, the roots of grace spreading far and wide, until Thou alone art seen in me, Thy beauty golden like summer harvest, Thy fruitfulness as the plenty of autumn." The preparation of our hearts should precede any request.

B. Some Examples of Confession (see pp. 36-37)

That Paul confessed his sin is implied in his deep awareness of sin (Rom. 7:7-25). In fact, he considered himself the chief of sinners and one who was totally unworthy to preach (1 Tim. 1:13, 15). Confession should be a daily part of our lives as well. Daily confession opens up the possibility of full fellowship through prayer. In Daniel's life there were probably times of special confession, as in chapter 9. But that doesn't mean he didn't confess his sin on a regular basis, waiting only for crises to come. We're often guilty of that, however. Rather than dealing with our sin on a regular basis, we allow it to accumulate until we arrive at communion or until disaster comes. Then, suddenly, we are eager to confess. But Daniel confessed his sin daily.

There were undoubtedly times in Daniel's life, however, when unusual events stimulated a greater sense of sinfulness. Scripture records several such confessions of sin, produced by monumental events. The Day of Atonement, also known as Yom Kippur, was a day of tremendous confession when the sins of all the nation were atoned (Lev. 16:21). It was not a substitute for daily confession but in addition to it. In the context of Hezekiah's great revival there was an outpouring of confession (2 Chron. 29:6). Later in the life of Israel, John the Baptist arrived, declaring that the Messiah was coming. He called for the people to confess their sins in repentance and to bring forth fruits of such repentance (Matt. 3:6, 8).

C. An Examination of Confession

Daniel's realization that Israel's seventy years of captivity were almost over was the occasion of his confession.

46

1. Daniel's confession (9:5-15; see pp. 37-40)

Repeatedly Daniel speaks of Israel's sin in his prayer. The essence of Daniel's confession was that Israel deserved the judgment she was receiving. One element of true confession is an acknowledgment of my sinfulness so the Lord can purify me, and so when God chastens me, I admit that I deserve it.

On one of the occasions that it was necessary to discipline one of my children, I asked her, "Do you know why I had to do that?" She said yes and then expressed her love to me with a kiss and a hug. She knew I had done justly, and that she was merely reaping the fruits of her misbehavior. In a sense when we confess to God, we free Him to chasten us without accusing Him of inequity or injustice.

Lesson

2. Other confessions

   a) Joshua 7:19-26

   God had commanded the Israelites not to take anything out of Jericho for themselves while conquering it (6:18-19). But Achan brought some things back and buried them under his tent. After the Lord revealed to Joshua that Achan was the one who had disobeyed (7:11-18), he confronted him.

   "Joshua said unto Achan, My son, give I pray thee, glory to the Lord God of Israel, and make confession unto him, and tell me now what thou hast done; hide it not from me. And Achan answered Joshua, and said, Indeed, I have sinned against the Lord God of Israel, and thus and thus have I done: When I saw among the spoils a beautiful Babylonish garment, and two hundred shekels of silver, and a wedge of gold of fifty shekels weight, then I coveted them, and took them; and, behold, they are hidden in the earth in the midst of my tent, and the silver under it. So Joshua sent messengers and they ran into the tent; and, behold, it was hidden in his tent, and the silver under it. And they took them out of the midst of the tent, and brought them unto Joshua, and unto all the children of Israel, and laid them out before the Lord. And Joshua, and all the children of Israel with him, took Achan, the son of Zerah, and the silver, and the garment, and the wedge of gold, and his sons, and his daughters, and his oxen, and his asses, and his sheep, and his tent, and all that he had; and they brought them unto the valley of Achor. And Joshua said, Why hast thou troubled us? The Lord shall trouble thee this day. And all Israel stoned him with stones, and burned them with fire, after they had stoned them with stones. And they raised over him a great heap of stones unto this day. So the Lord turned from the fierceness of his anger. Wherefore the name of that place was called, The valley of Achor [trouble], unto this day" (vv. 19-26).

If someone reading through the book of Joshua read that account without Joshua's confrontation and Achan's confession, they might wonder what kind of God would be so severe as to execute Achan, his children, and even his livestock. The Israelites even burned up his tent so that every remnant of the man's life was eliminated! Without reading verses 19-20, the incident loses its meaning and causes us to believe that God was unjust and inequitable. When Achan confessed, saying, "I have sinned" (v. 20), he admitted that he deserved to die. Scripture clearly states that sin results in death: "For the wages of sin is death" (Rom. 6:23). God said to Adam, "But of the tree of knowledge of good and evil, thou shalt not eat of it; for in the day that thou eatest thereof thou shalt surely die" (Gen. 2:17). The Lord spoke through Ezekiel, saying, "The soul that sinneth, it shall die" (Ezek. 18:20).

Confession of sin accomplishes two things: It brings about forgiveness of sin and frees God to chasten without any inequity by admitting that the punishment is deserved. That is precisely what Daniel was saying: "I know it's been a difficult seventy years under the Babylonian and Medo-Persian tyranny. Your people have suffered tremendously. But I still confess our sin, admitting that everything that has happened to us has been deserved because of our sin." Sometimes we wonder why things don't go the way we believe they should and why we don't receive what we believe we deserve. But if we received what we deserved, we would have died long ago. Our ability to take another breath is of the grace of God. We must acknowledge our sinfulness to free God from any injustice that we might wrongly attribute to Him.

b) 1 Samuel 4-6

(1) The context

The Philistines and Israelites were in a battle, and the Israelites were losing. Afraid of total defeat, someone said, "We need God!" (4:3). The Israelites hadn't sought God for a long time, but suddenly they decided they wanted God on their side. Because God's presence was represented by the Ark of the Covenant, they sent for it (4:4). When the Ark arrived, the Philistines heard Israel's shouting and became afraid, saying, "God is come into the camp. . . . Woe unto us! Who shall deliver us out of the hand of these mighty gods? These are the gods that smote the Egyptians with all the plagues in the wilderness" (4:7-8).

(2) The capture

The Hebrews were thrilled, believing that God had arrived and the victory was theirs. They apparently believed that God was like a genie. But they were mistaken. They had not lived righteously, and God would not come to their rescue. The fighting continued, and—probably to both sides' amazement—Israel lost (4:10). In addition, the Philistines captured the Ark (v. 11). The Philistines then had God on their hands!

(3) The consequences

(*a*) The destruction of Dagon

First Samuel 5:1-2 says, "The Philistines took the ark of God, and brought it from Ebenezer unto Ashdod. When the Philistines took the ark of God, they brought it into the house of Dagon, and set it by Dagon." In the temple of Dagon, who was represented by an idol that was half fish and half man, the Philistines placed what they believed to be the God of the Israelites. "When they of Ashdod arose early on the next day, behold, Dagon was fallen upon his face to the earth before the ark of the Lord. And they took Dagon, and set him in his place again. And when they arose early on the next morning, behold, Dagon was fallen upon his face to the ground before the ark of the Lord; and the head of Dagon and both palms of his hands were cut off upon the threshold; only the stump of Dagon was left to him" (vv. 3-4). God miraculously showed that He alone was God and that He wouldn't tolerate any competition. As a result, verse 5 says that no one in Ashdod ever worshiped Dagon again.

(*b*) The punishment of the Philistines

Verse 6 says, "The hand of the Lord was heavy upon them of Ashdod, and he destroyed them, and smote them with tumors." Though the King James Version says "emerods" (archaic form of hemorrhoids), the best translation is "tumors." Verse 9 says that "they had tumors in their secret [internal] parts."

The people of Ashdod wanted to get rid of the Ark because it was bringing them a terrible plague (v. 7). So they took the Ark to Gath (the home of Goliath), and the people there began to have tumors also (vv. 8-9). The people of Gath took it to Ekron, and the same thing happened (vv. 10-11). No one wanted the Ark. The Philistines had a meeting to determine how to get it back to the Israelites. They had been greatly afflicted by tumors and many had died in a plague brought by mice, possibly the bubonic plague or black death (v. 12; cf. 6:5).

(4) The confession

First Samuel 6:1-3 says, "The ark of the Lord was in the country of the Philistines seven months. And the Philistines called for the priests and the diviners, saying, What shall we do to the ark of the Lord? Tell us in what way we shall send it to its place. And they said, If ye send away the ark of the God of Israel, send it not empty; but by all means return him a trespass offering" (6:1-3). What does a trespass offering admit? Sin. Even pagans realized that all that had happened to them was their fault. They weren't like those in the future Tribulation who, when they are scorched with fire, curse God and blaspheme His name (Rev. 16:9). On the contrary, the Philistines were saying in effect, "We have offended God, and we need to make it right. We're receiving what we deserve."

Verse 4 continues, "Then said they, What shall be the trespass offering which we shall return to him? They answered, Five golden tumors, and five golden mice." Pagans often replicated a disease in clay, wood, or metal and offered it to their god as an affirmation that they knew the plague had come from that deity. In ancient Corinth, where Asklepios (or Asclepius), the god of healing, was worshiped, people would make

51

models of whatever part of their bodies they thought was healed by the god (Alice Walton, *The Cult of Asklepios* [New York: Ginn, 1894], pp. 57-58). The priests and diviners told the Philistines that they could appease Israel's God only in this way: "Wherefore ye shall make images of your tumors, and images of your mice that mar the land; and ye shall give glory unto the God of Israel. Perhaps he will lighten his hand from you, and from your gods, and from your land" (v. 5). The Philistines had to admit that the plague was their fault.

One of the essential elements of confession is recognizing that we have offended a holy God. If things aren't right in our lives, it's because we have brought it upon ourselves; God is righteous and therefore must chasten unrighteousness. It's only His grace that keeps us from being consumed in wrath.

Daniel acknowledged that Israel deserved her seventy-year captivity because of the sins of her people. He summed up his confession in verses 15-16: "We have sinned, we have done wickedly. O Lord, according to all thy righteousness, I beseech thee, let thine anger and thy fury be turned away from thy city, Jerusalem, thy holy mountain; because for our sins, and for the iniquities of our fathers, Jerusalem and thy people are become a reproach to all that are about us."

VII. PRAYER IS DEPENDENT ON GOD'S CHARACTER (vv. 4, 7, 9, 15)

If God were like the gods of the Philistines, it would be futile to ask for forgiveness, because their gods were evil and cruel. But our God is different: We confess our sins and intercede for the needs of others because God hears and responds. All prayer, then, is based on the character of God.

A. God's Character Displayed in Daniel's Prayer

In Daniel's prayer he recognized several of God's attributes.

1. Power (v. 4*a-b*)

   "I prayed unto the Lord, my God, and made my confession, and said, O Lord, the great . . . God."

   The word *great* means "powerful." Daniel prayed to God because He is powerful enough to respond. He can change the circumstances. He proved He has infinite resources at His disposal when he brought His "people forth out of the land of Egypt with a mighty hand" (v. 15). God is powerful.

2. Majesty (v. 4*b*)

   "The . . . awesome God."

   "Awesome" speaks of majesty and implies that God is to be honored and glorified—for He alone is worthy.

3. Faithfulness (v. 4*c*)

   "Keeping the covenant."

   When God makes a promise, He keeps it. He made a covenant with His people that He would never forsake them (Deut. 31:6; cf. Heb. 6:13-18). If they repented He would forgive them. If they obeyed He would restore them (Deut. 30:1-3). God spoke through Jeremiah, saying, "Call unto me, and I will answer thee, and show thee great and mighty things which thou knowest not" (Jer. 33:3). The Bible also says that if our hearts are pure and our sins are forsaken when we call upon His name, He will respond (Ps. 34:15-22).

   We pray not only because we believe God has the power to fulfill our requests, and because He is the most majestic Being in the universe, but also because He is faithful to keep His promises.

4. Love (v. 4*d*)

   "Mercy to them that love him."

The word *mercy* is an expression of God's love—He forgives because He loves. He will grant us what we ask in His will because He loves us (John 15:7-9). God's faithfulness is encompassed by His love (Ps. 89:33; Jer. 31:3).

5. Holiness (v. 7a)

"O Lord, righteousness belongeth unto thee."

God is holy and therefore does what is right. How wonderful to know that God always is right, never making a mistake (Gen. 18:25; Deut. 32:4).

6. Forgiveness (v. 9a)

"To the Lord, our God, belong mercies and forgiveness."

God is merciful and forgiving. God's forgiveness appears in the plural in this verse, indicating that it is not easily exhausted. God's abundant forgiveness and mercy show that He is a gracious God.

B. God's Character Displayed in the Cross

When we look at the cross, we see those same attributes expressed there.

1. Power

On the cross Christ conquered sin, death, and Satan —now that's power (Heb. 2:14-15; 1 John 3:8)!

2. Majesty

Although Christ appeared to be a victim of the Romans and the Jewish leaders, He controlled everything that happened on the way to the cross (John 10:15-18; 19:28-30). The centurion who guarded Jesus witnessed that majesty and uttered in absolute astonishment, "Truly, this was the Son of God" (Matt. 27:54). He was majestic even in His death.

3. Faithfulness

Christ said that it was necessary for Him to go to the cross (Matt. 26:2). Although He agonized about it in the Garden of Gethsemane, He faithfully kept His promise and was submissive to His Father's will (Matt. 26:39, 42).

4. Love

I see Christ's love at the cross because He shouldn't have been there—I should have (Mark 10:45; 1 Pet. 3:18). Because He loves me, He took my place.

5. Holiness

The holiness of God put Christ on the cross. He couldn't arbitrarily forgive sinners. Christ had to pay for sin because God cannot tolerate sin—its penalty must be paid (Col. 1:19-22).

6. Forgiveness

Finally, we see Christ's mercy and forgiveness on the cross. He bore every sin of everyone who has ever lived so He could give those who receive Him the gift of salvation (Eph. 1:7; 2:8).

All that God was to Daniel, He is to us as well. Daniel saw God's character in His dealings with Israel; we see it in the cross. We can commune through prayer with a God who is powerful, majestic, faithful, loving, holy, and gracious.

VIII. PRAYER CONSUMMATES IN GOD'S GLORY (vv. 16-19)

A. Illustrated by Daniel (9:16-19)

Daniel prayed, "O Lord, according to all thy righteousness, I beseech thee, let thine anger and thy fury be turned away from thy city, Jerusalem, thy holy mountain; because for our sins, and for the iniquities of our fathers, Jerusalem and thy people are become a reproach to all that are about us. Now, therefore, O our God, hear the prayer of thy servant, and his supplications, and cause thy face to shine upon thy sanctuary that is desolate, for the Lord's sake. O my God, incline thine ear, and hear; open thine eyes, and behold our desolations, and the city which is called by thy name; for we do not present our supplications before thee for our righteousness, but for thy great mercies. O Lord, hear; O Lord, forgive; O Lord, hearken and do; defer not, for thine own sake, O my God; for thy city and thy people are called by thy name" (vv. 16-19).

Because the captivity of Judah and the destruction of its Temple were interpreted by the nations around it as an indication that Judah's God was either powerless or non-existent, Daniel was saying, "God, vindicate Your name. Don't let Your name be slandered. Don't let our sin corrupt Your reputation." That is a mature prayer—"Forgive us for Your sake." People today tend to pray only for their own desires, forgetting that God is to be glorified.

Jeremiah had prophesied concerning the destruction of the land: "Thus saith the Lord of hosts, Behold, I will send upon them the sword, the famine, and the pestilence, and will make them like vile figs, that cannot be eaten, they are so bad. And I will persecute them with the sword, with the famine, and with the pestilence, and will deliver them to be removed to all the kingdoms of the earth, to be a curse, and an horror, and an hissing, and a reproach, among all the nations to which I have driven them, because they have not hearkened to my words, saith the Lord, which I sent unto them by my servants, the prophets, rising up early and sending them; but ye would not hear, saith the Lord." God said He was going to judge Israel for a period of time because of its evil. But in response to the prophecy Daniel pleaded, "God, don't prolong it; we are a hissing among the nations, and Your reputation is at stake because we bear Your name."

B. Illustrated by the Psalmist (102:12-19)

The psalmist said, "Thou, O Lord, shalt endure forever, and thy remembrance unto all generations. Thou shalt arise, and have mercy upon Zion; for the time to favor her, yea, the set time, is come. For thy servants take pleasure in her stones, and favor the dust thereof. So the nations shall fear the name of the Lord, and all the kinds of the earth thy glory. When the Lord shall build up Zion, he shall appear in his glory. He will regard the prayer of the destitute, and not despise their prayer. This shall be written for the generation to come; and the people who shall be created shall praise the Lord. For he hath looked down from the height of his sanctuary; from heaven did the Lord behold the earth." The psalmist was saying that when God rebuilds His city, people will say that He is great. Do you pray that God will do certain things in your life and in the lives of others that He might be glorified?

Conclusion

Daniel prayed that God would forgive Judah's sins, which were a reproach upon His name. He desired that God restore the virtue, holiness, and majesty of His name in the eyes of the world. The severest consequence of my sin is that it brings reproach upon the perfect character of God, whose name I bear. If we were trying to protect only our own reputations, we would be more susceptible to sin. But with God's reputation at stake, we must be careful to live holy lives.

We have seen that prayer is generated by the Word of God, grounded in the will of God, characterized by fervency, realized in self-denial, identified with others, strengthened in confession, dependent on God's character, and consummated in God's glory. That kind of prayer gets an answer from God. When Daniel prayed like that, he received an answer that could be the most glorious prophecy in the book of Daniel (9:20-27).

Focusing on the Facts

1. Prayer is primarily _____ with God (see p. 44).
2. What does confession mean (see p. 45)?
3. What should be our attitude when we enter the presence of God in prayer (see p. 45)?
4. Of what are we often guilty with regard to confession (see p. 46)?

5. How can we free God to chasten without accusing Him of inequity or injustice (see p. 47)?
6. When Achan confessed, what did he admit (Josh. 7:20; see p. 48)?
7. What verse explains the consequences of sin (see p. 48)?
8. What two things does confession of sin accomplish (see pp. 48-49)?
9. If God gave us what we deserved, what would it be (see p. 49; cf. Rom. 6:23; 9:29)?
10. Why wasn't God obligated to come to Israel's rescue in 1 Samuel 4 (see p. 49)?
11. How did God show the people of Ashdod that He wouldn't tolerate any competition (see p. 50)?
12. What did the Philistines show that they realized by offering a trespass offering to God (see p. 51)?
13. If God were like the gods of the Philistines, would it be futile to ask God for forgiveness? Why (see p. 52)?
14. What motivates us to confess our sins and intercede for others (see p. 52)?
15. Daniel acknowledged God's power in his prayer. What incident in Israel's history did he cite as a demonstration of God's power (Dan. 9:15; see pp. 52-53)?
16. What attribute of God is demonstrated by God's keeping His promises (see p. 53)?
17. How does the cross of Christ demonstrate the power of God? His faithfulness? His love (see pp. 54-55)?
18. What attribute of God demanded Christ's death on the cross? Why (see p. 55)?
19. Whose reputation was ultimately at stake as a result of Israel's sinfulness (see p. 56)?
20. What is the severest consequence of sin (see p. 57)?

Pondering the Principles

1. If you are aware of some sinful thought, word, or deed in your life that you haven't confessed, why haven't you been willing to bring it to God? Are you afraid to ask for God's forgiveness again, or are you waiting until some crisis comes? Read what 1 John 1:6-9 says about sin and what we should do about it. What is the basis of our cleansing from sin (v. 7)? What do verses 8 and 10 say that we do to ourselves and God when we deny that we have committed sin or have a sin nature? What are the re-

sults of confessing our sins (v. 9)? Look at the consequences of failing to confess our sins (see Ps. 32:3-4; 66:18; Isa. 1:15-16; 1 Cor. 11:28-32). Read the great assurance that we are given in 1 John 2:1-2. Next read Psalm 103:8-13, thanking God for what He says about our sins.

2. Are you growing "in grace, and in the knowledge of our Lord and Saviour, Jesus Christ" (2 Pet. 3:18)? Or do you find yourself lacking the Christian virtues found in 2 Peter 1:5-7, becoming spiritually insensitive like the one who "hath forgotten that he was purged from his old sins" (v. 9)? The apostle Paul exhorts us to "examine [ourselves], whether [we] are in the faith" (2 Cor. 13:5). He cautions us against deceiving ourselves and believing we are Christians merely because we associate with other Christians and do what they do. Do you know the truth but refuse to respond to it? Or are you learning more about the nature and power of God and responding in an appropriate way? Is your faith in God general faith that acts upon what it believes, or are you like the man Christ described who built a beautiful house of external religion—but who built on the sand rather than the rock of obedience (Matt. 7:26-27)?

4
Prayer as Worship

Outline

Introduction
A. The Perversion of Self-Indulgent Prayer
B. The Focus of Biblical Prayer
   1. Explained
   2. Illustrated
     a) Jeremiah
     b) Daniel
     c) Jonah

Lesson
  I. Pray with an Awareness of God's Paternity (v. 9*b*)
    A. Misconceptions of God's Character
      1. The Stoics' view
      2. The Epicureans' view
    B. Ramifications of God's Paternity
 II. Pray for the Realization of God's Priority (v. 9*c*)
    A. Understanding God's Priority
    B. Displaying God's Priority
III. Pray for the Advancement of God's Program (v. 10*a*)
    A. It Broadens Our Perspective
    B. It Builds the Kingdom
IV. Pray for the Accomplishment of God's Purpose (v. 10*b*)

Conclusion

Introduction

A. The Perversion of Self-Indulgent Prayer

As I examine what's happening in Christian circles, I see the steady growth of a movement that is a threat to the sanity and purity of the church—positive confession and the prosperity gospel. Certain Christian radio and television programs and even some churches are convincing people that prayer is simply a way to get what you want and that God is obligated to grant whatever you request. Although the Bible teaches that God is sovereign and man is His servant, the prosperity gospel implies the opposite: that man is a sovereign who makes demands and God is a servant who must deliver. We live in an indulgent, selfish, materialistic society, and the waves of that society have washed ashore on Christian theology. Teaching that says we can demand things of God is a spiritual justification for self-indulgence. It perverts prayer and takes the Lord's name in vain. It is unbiblical, ungodly, and is not directed by the Holy Spirit.

B. The Focus of Biblical Prayer

1. Explained

Because of so much false teaching, Christians need to reexamine how they should pray. The focal point of the Bible's instruction about how to pray is in Matthew 6. Jesus said, "After this manner, therefore, pray ye: Our Father, who art in heaven, hallowed be thy name. Thy kingdom come. Thy will be done in earth, as it is in heaven. Give us this day our daily bread. And forgive us our debts, as we forgive our debtors. And lead us not into temptation, but deliver us from evil. For thine is the kingdom, and the power, and the glory, forever. Amen" (vv. 9-13). From beginning to end that model prayer focuses on God—hallowing His name, praying that His kingdom would come, wanting His will to be done. Its few petitions conclude with a benediction of praise to God. So the focus of biblical praying is the glory of God and the extension of His kingdom.

In John 14:13 Jesus says, "Whatever ye shall ask in my name, that will I do, that the Father may be glorified in the Son." Prayer begins and ends not with the needs of man but with the glory of God. It should be concerned primarily with who God is, what He wants, and how He can be glorified. Prayer that is selfishly motivated and makes demands of God does violence to God's name, His character, His will, and His Word. So when men demand things of God and say that He always wants His people to be healthy, wealthy, and successful, realize that they are not spiritual men. They aren't preoccupied with the extension of Christ's kingdom or the glory of God's name but with the extension of their own empire and the fulfillment of their own selfish desires. Every believer must understand that. Such teaching attacks the heart of Christian truth—the very character of God.

2. Illustrated

a) Jeremiah

In Jeremiah 32 Jeremiah was in prison. He was preaching to a nation of people who refused to hear him and were so antagonistic that they later threw him in a pit in an attempt to silence him. By human standards his ministry was a miserable failure.

But Jeremiah prayed, "Ah, Lord God! Behold, thou hast made the heaven and the earth by thy great power and outstretched arm, and there is nothing too hard for thee; thou showest loving-kindness unto thousands, and recompensest the iniquity of the fathers into the bosom of their children after them; the Great, the Mighty God, the Lord of hosts is his name, great in counsel, and mighty in work; for thine eyes are open upon all the ways of the sons of men, to give every one according to . . . the fruit of his doings; who hast set signs and wonders in the land of Egypt, even unto this day, and in Israel, and among other men; and hast made thee a name, as at this day; and hast brought forth thy people, Israel, out of the land of Egypt with signs, and with wonders, and with a strong hand, and with an outstretched arm, and with great terror; and hast given them this land, which thou didst swear to their fathers to give them, a land flowing with milk and honey; and they came in, and possessed it; but they obeyed not thy voice, neither walked in thy law; they have done nothing of all that thou commandedest them to do; therefore, thou hast caused all this evil to come upon them" (vv. 17-23).

Jeremiah was in great distress and loneliness. He could have despaired about his ministry, but he was engrossed in extolling the glory, name, and works of God. He wasn't preoccupied with his own painful circumstances.

b) Daniel

Daniel was also in a difficult situation. Caught in the transition between two great world empires, he was representing a captive nation in a foreign land. In Daniel 9 he says, "I set my face unto the Lord God, to seek by prayer and supplications, with fasting, and sackcloth and ashes; and I prayed unto the Lord, my God, and made my confession, and said, O Lord, the great and awesome God, keeping the covenant and mercy to them that love him, and to them that keep his commandments, we have sinned" (vv. 3-5). He began his prayer by affirming the nature and character of God.

c) Jonah

Recalling what happened while he was in the belly of the fish, Jonah said, "I remembered the Lord; and my prayer came in unto thee, into thine holy temple" (Jonah 2:7). Verse 9 mentions the content of his prayer: "I will sacrifice unto thee with the voice of thanksgiving; I will pay that that I have vowed. Salvation is of the Lord." That might seem like an unusual prayer when you're caught in the belly of a fish! There was no pleading, begging, or demanding. He simply extolled the character of God.

Lesson

Matthew 6:9-10 presents four elements of prayer that demonstrate it's an act of worship.

I. PRAY WITH AN AWARENESS OF GOD'S PATERNITY (v. 9*b*)

"Our Father, who art in heaven."

God is not only our King, our Judge, and our Creator but also our Father. That relationship gives us the freedom to enter His presence as a son would enter the presence of his earthly father. Isaiah 64:8 says, "O Lord, thou art our Father; we are the clay, and thou our potter, and we all are the work of thy hand." We recognize that God gave us life and that we belong to Him through faith in Christ. We are His children. When we come to God in prayer, we are speaking to our Father.

A. Misconceptions of God's Character

The pagans often worshiped violent, unjust, jealous gods whom they believed they had to appease. The Jewish people thought of God as their Father only in a national sense. Because they felt so distant from God and were so fearful of Him, they refused even to speak His name. Others in the Greco-Roman world created gods who were unconcerned with mankind.

1. The Stoics' view

The Stoics, a well-known group of philosophers in the Greek and Roman world, taught that one attribute all the gods shared was *apatheia*. Although the English word *apathy* comes from that word, its definition doesn't adequately define *apatheia*. The Greek word means "unable to experience any feelings." The Stoics taught that because man feels love and hate, joy and sorrow, contentment and anger, he is volatile. The problems of life are closely tied to man's ability to feel the range of emotions. Because they apparently wanted to set the gods apart from the struggle of man and make them greater than man, they concluded that the gods were *apatheia*—beyond feeling anything. But Jesus, who perfectly revealed God, said that He is a loving Father, who is not unfeeling or without emotion.

2. The Epicureans' view

The Epicureans taught that the primary attribute of the gods was *artaraxia*, which means "perfect peace" or "complete calm." They believed that if the gods became involved in human affairs, they would be unable to maintain their serenity. So the Epicureans inferred that the gods remained completely detached from the world. Christ entered that religious climate and spoke of the intimate relationship people can have with God. But the concept of an impersonal God continues to thrive. For example, Albert Einstein believed that some kind of cosmic force existed but believed it was impersonal and unknowable (Albert Einstein, *Cosmic Religion* [New York: Covici, Friede, 1931], pp. 47-48). But by His life Christ revealed that God experiences the full range of human emotion.

B. Ramifications of God's Paternity

1. It dispels fear

Jesus Christ made us acceptable to God, so we are no longer afraid of Him. He has adopted us into His family. One of the most famous Greek myths concerned Prometheus, a descendant of the Titans. When he saw that man's life was difficult and dangerous, in pity he took fire from the realm of the gods and gave it to man. Zeus, the supreme ruler of the gods, was furious; he wanted to keep man in a helpless and humble state. So Zeus had Prometheus chained to a rock where he was constantly exposed to the elements. In addition, Zeus sent an eagle to gnaw on his liver. Every night his liver replenished itself, and every day the eagle returned to devour it. That story is a graphic illustration of the typical nature of the false gods of false religions—they're vengeful and jealous, and man must take desperate measures to appease them. But knowing that the true God is our Father dispels all fear.

2. It encourages hope

If we ask our Father for bread, He won't give us a stone. If we ask Him for a fish, He won't give us a snake (Luke 11:11-13). Whatever His children ask that fits within His will, He grants. We can live in hope in this world because we know our God is a loving Father.

3. It removes loneliness

Although we may not have a friend in the world, He is our friend (John 15:15). He is a Father who will never leave us or forsake us (Heb. 13:5). God's presence is all a believer needs to drive away loneliness.

4. It defeats selfishness

Notice Christ's use of plural pronouns: "our Father" (v. 9), "our daily bread" (v. 11), "our debts" and "our debtors" (v. 12), and "deliver us from evil" (v. 13). His point is that we have brothers and sisters in Christ who are also children of God. So whatever we ask must include them as well. We shouldn't ask God to give us what we want without caring how others will be affected. In my family we try to do things that benefit each member. If one child wants something special, we usually consider giving it only if we can do something equally as special for the other children. Part of being a parent is realizing that no child exists in isolation from the others—all are part of the family. So our prayers shouldn't be filled with selfish requests. We should ask God to do what is best for us in the context of His entire family.

5. It provides resources

God is "in heaven." He's not bound to earth or subject to our limitations. The natural resources of the earth are diminishing. According to the law of entropy—the second law of thermodynamics—everything is moving toward a state of disorder or degradation. We are constantly exhausting our resources. But there is no shortage of spiritual resources. God pours them out on us, and they are never exhausted. Because God is in heaven, He is not bound by the diminishing resources of this world. He makes everything we need available to us.

6. It insures wisdom

The old saying "Father knows best" definitely applies to our heavenly Father. Because He is perfect, He does know best.

7. It demands obedience

An integral part of the father/child relationship is obedience. Jesus illustrated that truth personally as He, the Son of God, submitted to the Father.

When we pray "our Father," we're acknowledging that we are God's children, that He loves us, and that we have intimate access to Him. We are recognizing that He has unlimited resources, that His family is larger than just one individual, that He will do whatever is best for us, and that we need to obey Him.

II. PRAY FOR THE REALIZATION OF GOD'S PRIORITY (v. 9c)

"Hallowed be thy name."

A. Understanding God's Priority

Our first concern in prayer should be that God's name be hallowed. Commentator Arthur W. Pink said, "How clearly, then, is the fundamental duty in prayer here set forth: self and all its needs must be given a secondary place and the Lord freely accorded the preeminence in our thoughts, desires, and supplications. This petition must take the precedence, for the glory of God's great name is the ultimate end of all things" (*An Exposition of the Sermon on the Mount* [Grand Rapids: Baker, 1974], pp. 161-62). In biblical times a person's name represented all that he was. That's still true to an extent. My name is more than just a name; it sums up who I am. God's name stands for His nature, attributes, character, and personality. "To hallow" means "to set apart as sacred." The normal Greek word meaning "to treat as sacred" or "to hallow" (*hagiazō*) can be clarified by a synonym (*daxazō*), which means "to glorify" or "to honor." So when we pray that God's name would be hallowed, we are asking that God be glorified. Although the kind of praying that is popular today continually begs for more possessions, prosperity, and success, biblical prayer seeks God's glory.

How to Avoid Being Sentimental Toward God

When the purpose of our prayers is that God be glorified and exalted, we protect ourselves against the sentimentalism that can develop from referring to God only as "our Father." It is easy for Christians to magnify the concept of God's Fatherhood and forget the balancing truth of His greatness. The Jewish people, when referring to God as Father, tended to add some expression of His power. For example, in the daily benedictions, sometimes referred to as *Shemoneh Esreh*, they repeated, "With great love hast Thou loved us, O Lord our God, and with much overflowing pity hast Thou pitied us, our Father and our King" (Alfred Edersheim, *Sketches of Jewish Social Life* [Grand Rapids: Eerdmans, 1972], p. 269). God is not only our Father; He is also our King. And His name should be exalted and glorified in every way.

B. Displaying God's Priority

Our prayers exalt God's name when we pray that He would do that which brings Him glory. Whether we are praying about a child, a job, or a physical problem, our prayer should be that God will do whatever lifts up His name, whatever causes people to recognize Him as the true God.

The god of the contemporary name-it-and-claim-it theology, who obeys everyone's commands, is not the true God. When Christians demand things from God, they slander Him rather than exalt Him. Such praying strikes at His very nature. It isn't merely bad doctrine; it is gross irreverence.

Martin Luther's larger catechism on this phrase of the Lord's Prayer asks, "How is God's name hallowed amongst us?" His answer: "When both our doctrine and our life are godly and Christian." So God is glorified when we believe rightly about Him and live rightly in submission to Him. Praying "hallowed be thy name" is essentially asking God to put Himself on display in our lives whether in poverty or wealth, sickness or health, life or death.

Fourth-century bishop Gregory of Nyssa (a city in Asia Minor) well described the kind of person who hallows God's name: "He touches the earth but lightly with the tip of his toes, for he is not engulfed by the pleasurable enjoyments of its life, but is above all deceit that comes by the senses. And so, even though in the flesh, he strives after the immaterial life. He counts the possession of virtues the only riches, familiarity with God the only nobility. His only privilege and power is the mastery of self so as not to be a slave of human passions. He is saddened if his life in this material world be prolonged; like those who are seasick he hastens to reach the port of rest" (*St. Gregory of Nyssa*, translated by Hilda C. Graef [Westminster, Md.: Newman, 1954], p. 50). The man who hallows God's name is more concerned about the glory of God than his own circumstances, reputation, or prosperity. He is more offended by what dishonors God than how he himself is being treated. Psalm 34:3, summarizing that aspect of prayer, says, "Oh, magnify the Lord with me, and let us exalt his name together."

III. PRAY FOR THE ADVANCEMENT OF GOD'S PROGRAM (v. 10*a*)

"Thy kingdom come."

Every true man of God throughout history has been consumed with the advancement of God's kingdom, not the building of his own empire or the growth of his bank balance.

How to Evaluate the Character of a Christian Leader

How can we evaluate the character of a well-known Christian leader whom we don't know personally? There are two helpful questions to ask. First, if he's attained a level of leadership where many people work around him, how long do the godly ones continue working with him? That's an accurate measure of his character, because if workers stay with him, they have found him to be of like mind.

Second, how much of his success accumulates in his own pocket? If after much success a man hasn't indulged himself excessively, apparently his preoccupation isn't building his bank account but building the kingdom.

A. It Broadens Our Perspective

In my prayers I shouldn't be concerned with how something will affect the enterprise and efforts of John MacArthur, but how it will affect the expansion of the kingdom. The Talmud implies that a prayer that doesn't mention the kingdom of God is no prayer at all (*Berakoth* 21*a*). At the heart of every petition should be a concern for how it will advance the kingdom. Although we should pray for our own families and needs, and for our local and national leadership, that shouldn't be the sum of our prayers. We need to see the big picture, so we should pray for the growth of God's kingdom and not our petty kingdom. That perspective is indispensable in the ministry. You don't pray just for your church, your radio ministry, your college and seminary. But you pray that God's kingdom would advance however and through whomever God wills.

B. It Builds the Kingdom

The kingdom of God is the sphere of salvation Christ rules over. Although God has been, is, and will continue to be the sovereign Ruler of everything in the universe, the kingdom that Christ refers to in Matthew 6:10 is more specific. During His earthly ministry Christ said, "The kingdom is in the midst of you" (Luke 17:21). Christ rules in the heart of everyone who has put his faith in Him. He is the Lord and King of every believer—that's His kingdom. However, in the future Christ will establish a literal kingdom on earth, a reign that the Bible says will last a thousand years. Then in eternity His kingdom will encompass the entire universe. Our prayer should be for whatever advances His kingdom—for the salvation of the lost and for Christ to return and establish His earthly kingdom. We should also pray that God would advance the elements of the kingdom mentioned in Romans 14:17, where Paul says, "The Kingdom of God is . . . righteousness, and peace, and joy in the Holy Spirit."

Unfortunately, today's popular concept of prayer is so egocentric that some Christians only consider themselves and what they want. They tend to overlook the greater cause of God's kingdom. Our prayer should be, "Lord, expand your kingdom even if it means I lose everything." Eighteenth-century hymn writer Frances Havergal wrote the following words to Christ in "His Coming to Glory":

> Oh the joy to see Thee reigning,
> Thee, my own beloved Lord!
> Every tongue Thy name confessing,
> Worship, honor, glory, blessing
> Brought to Thee with glad accord;
> Thee, my Master and my Friend,
> Vindicated and enthroned;
> Unto earth's remotest end
> Glorified, adored, and owned.

Worship is at the heart of biblical praying. We pray to a loving Father, accepting His wisdom and responding with obedience. A desire for God to be glorified and His kingdom extended should permeate our prayers.

IV. PRAY FOR THE ACCOMPLISHMENT OF GOD'S PURPOSE
(v. 10b)

"Thy will be done in earth, as it is in heaven."

The Bible clearly teaches that God's will is done in heaven. Angels who refused to do His will were cast out of heaven with Lucifer, their leader. I pray asking the Lord to accomplish His purpose. Occasionally someone asks what would happen if the Lord suddenly took away my ministry. My response is that if that were God's will, I would accept it. Although overwhelmed with personal disaster, Job was able to say, "The Lord gave, and the Lord hath taken away; blessed be the name of the Lord" (Job 1:21). Others often ask about my goals for ministry. I don't have a personal agenda; I just want to do God's will daily.

Some Christians accept God's will with a spirit of resignation and bitterness. Eleventh-century Persian poet Omar Khayyam had that perspective of God. In verse 69 of the *Rubaiyat*, a collection of his four-lined epigrams, he said:

> But helpless Pieces of the Game He plays
> Upon this Checkerboard of Nights and Days;
> Hither and thither moves, and checks, and slays,
> And one by one back in the Closet lays.

What a tragic view of God! So some people grit their teeth and resentfully say, "Thy will be done." Others passively resign themselves, at the same time complaining about the tragedy of their circumstances. The hyper-Calvinist's theology greatly colors his perspective. He resigns himself fatalistically to his circumstances since God is more powerful than he is and everything will happen as planned. But saying "Thy will be done" doesn't mean giving up.

Professor David Wells defined petitionary prayer as "rebellion—rebellion against the world in its fallenness, the absolute and undying refusal to accept as normal what is pervasively abnormal. It is, in this its negative aspect, the refusal of every agenda, every scheme, every interpretation that is at odds with the norm as originally established by God" ("Prayer: Rebelling Against the Status Quo," *Christianity Today*, [2 November 1979]: 33). We don't have to accept the evil that's around us or God's name being dishonored. We can pray like those who will be slain for their testimony during the Great Tribulation: "How long, O Lord, holy and true, dost thou not judge and avenge our blood on them that dwell on the earth" (Rev. 6:10). We can plead with God to act because He is being dishonored. We can ask Him to change the circumstances to bring honor to His name. But whatever God brings we have to accept as His will, knowing that it's His best. Sometimes it may not seem to be the best to us, but that's because we can't see the big picture.

Conclusion

Because God is our loving Father, He won't give us a stone when we ask for bread or a snake when we ask for fish. He will meet the needs of His children with His unlimited resources. But behind everything God does are His immutable purposes: glorifying His name, extending His kingdom, and fulfilling His will. So our prayers must be motivated and controlled by those purposes. The goal of prayer is not so much getting answers as deepening our dependency on Him and being a part of what He is doing. Only when our prayers demonstrate the attitudes found in the first two verses of the Lord's Prayer are we ready to ask God to supply our daily needs (v. 11), to cleanse us from sin (v. 12), and to protect us (v. 13a). But our petitions must remain within the context of His glory (v. 13b).

Any prayer that doesn't worship God by seeking His glory and the expansion of His kingdom isn't prayer at all—it's an exercise in self-indulgence. Any theology that assumes God has to give us whatever we demand dishonors God by making man the sovereign and God the servant. Jesus taught us how to pray so that God might be glorified.

Focusing on the Facts

1. How has the prosperity gospel affected prayer (see p. 62)?
2. What is the focus of biblical prayer (see p. 62)?
3. What does John 14:13 teach about prayer (see p. 63)?
4. Explain how Jeremiah illustrates the proper focus of prayer (see p. 64).
5. Did the Jewish people think of God as their Father? Explain (see p. 65).
6. Who were the Stoics? What was their misconception of God (see pp. 65-66)?
7. What did the Epicureans believe was the primary attribute of the gods (see p. 66)?
8. Explain the ramifications of God's being our Father (see pp. 66-68).
9. What does "hallowed be thy name" mean (see pp. 68-69)?
10. How can Christians hallow God's name (see pp. 69-70)?
11. What two questions will help us evaluate the character of Christian leaders (see pp. 70-71)?
12. What should be at the heart of every petition (see p. 71)?
13. What is the kingdom of God (see p. 71)?
14. _____ is at the heart of biblical praying (see p. 72).

15. Can a believer accept God's will with an improper attitude? Explain (see p. 73).
16. How did David Wells define petitionary prayer (see p. 73)?
17. What was Christ's purpose in teaching us how to pray (see p. 74)?

Pondering the Principles

1. No aspect of prayer is more important—or more neglected—than worship. When we finally take time from our overcrowded schedules to pray, too often we rush into God's presence, say a few words of thanksgiving, make our urgent requests, and quickly exit to the busyness of living. Rather than being the exception, such a scenario has become the rule for many Christians. Others make praying for their requests a priority but still neglect to worship God. Worship is at the heart of biblical praying. And when we neglect it, our relationship with God suffers. How committed are you to worshiping God in prayer? Take time now to pray. This time don't allow yourself to mention any requests to God. Instead concentrate on worshiping Him. Begin making worship a vital part of your prayers.

2. Someone once said that every virtue has the potential for becoming a vice. That is certainly true of our commitment to a particular Christian ministry. Immersing ourselves in ministry at church or in some other Christian organization is commendable, but if we fail to guard our thinking, our perspective can narrow until we forget that our ministry is merely a part of what God is doing. We can become arrogant and begin to feel we are competing with others who are serving the Lord. Eventually we could cause division and factions within Christ's Body. Do you have the big picture? Do you understand that your ministry is one small part of God's kingdom? To regain a balanced perspective about what God is doing, read Ephesians 2:11–4:16. Ask God to give you the grace to want His kingdom to advance, regardless of what happens to you and your ministry.

Scripture Index

Topical Index